Sustainable Organizations
Empowering Employees to Make Green Decisions

Table of Contents

Chapter 1. Introduction

In the vast tapestry of today's corporate landscape, Sustainable Organizations hold a brilliant hue. Our Special Report takes you on an enthralling journey through workplaces of the future, where employees are not just involved, but actually empowered to make eco-friendly decisions. This is not just about plots and policies, but a narrative of change, innovation, and harmonizing business growth with environmental sustainability. Step into the world of dynamic dialogues on green decisions and innovative strategies. No techno-jargon, we promise; just enriching, inspiring tales that illuminate how empowering employees can catalyze eco-consciousness, and why it pays to play green. If you're eager to be part of the transformative path towards a sustainable future, this Special Report is the perfect read! With curiosity as your guide, let's explore how sustainable organizations are paving the way to a greener future!

Chapter 2. Laying the Foundation: The Basics of Sustainable Organizations

The remarkable potential for Sustainable Organizations begins with an understanding of its fundamental principles. Driven by innovation, environmental conscientiousness and employee empowerment, these virtuous companies demonstrate that environmental business isn't just a responsibility – it can be a powerful pathway for enhanced productivity, innovation, work-place satisfaction, and meaningful change.

2.1. Foundations of Sustainable Organizations

The concept of a Sustainable Organization may seem somewhat abstract to some. So first, let's appreciate it in the simplest terms. A Sustainable Organization is one that respects the triple bottom line – People, Planet, and Profit. It's an organization that, beyond economic success, is multifaceted in its commitment to environmental protection and societal responsibility. This is about achieving long-term durable growth while minimizing the negative impact on the environment and maximizing value for stakeholders, including employees, customers and society at large.

It incorporates a deep understanding that the organization, its environment, and the society in which it operates are interconnected. Only by taking a holistic view to balance economic, social, and environmental needs can a modern organization strive for sustainability.

Sustainable Organizations adapt their business strategies and operating models to create value that extends beyond immediate short-term financial gains. They view their stakeholders as partners in their journey towards sustainability, involving them in decision-making processes.

2.2. Elements of a Sustainable Business Model

Sustainability isn't an over-night transformation. It involves a strategic shift in how a business operates. Some fundamental elements of a sustainable business model that are always kept at the forefront of such change include:

- Sticking to the triple bottom line principle, while maintaining productivity as their North Star.
- Committing to a culture of innovation to strive for sustainable alternatives in their business practices.
- Ensuring transparency in its operations to build trust with its stakeholders.
- Upholding ethical standards in all aspects of its operations.
- Creating a nurturing environment promoting employee engagement and empowerment.

But the one thread that ties all these elements together is the genuine understanding and integration of sustainability within the organization's culture. Without a culture that values and nurtures sustainable practices, even the most well-intended strategies can fail.

2.3. Strategies for a Sustainable Business Model

A Sustainable Organization constantly aligns its mission with the fundamental elements of sustainability, adapting it with shifting scenarios, and reflecting it in the strategies it employs. Some strategies could include:

- Incorporating sustainability right from product design to end-of-life solutions.

- Investing in technology that helps reduce carbon footprint.

- Using resources judiciously and advocating waste recycling.

- Ensuring fair-trade practices within their supply chain.

- Empowering employees to implement and brainstorm green initiatives.

2.4. The Role of Leadership in Sustainable Organizations

Leadership plays a critical role in driving sustainability. Leaders are the visionaries who determine the course of an organization. It is their commitment towards sustainability that can infuse it as an intrinsic part of the organization's identity.

Leaders in sustainable organizations, apart from driving the business towards profitability, must motivate and guide their teams to integrate sustainability into their daily workflows. They must highlight that sustainability isn't just desirable but achievable and beneficial.

These leaders set the tone and establish the value system in their organizations. They engage employees and stakeholders in dialogue around sustainability, ensure transparency, and challenge unfavourable traditions while fostering innovation and change. Empowered leadership is therefore an indispensable element of a Sustainable Organization.

2.5. Employee Participation in Sustainability

In sustainable organizations, employees aren't just workers—they are contributors to the sustainability initiative. It's through empowered employees that big changes happen on a daily basis. Employees are the direct executors of sustainability strategies who can innovate, reshape, and drive those small yet impactful changes that add up to a larger difference. With the right information and tools, they can actively participate in making decisions that align with the organization's sustainability pathway.

2.6. The Way Forward for Sustainable Organizations

Sustainability is a commitment to present and future generations. The practices, decisions, and innovations of today's Sustainable Organizations pave the way for a greener, cleaner future. More than just a business strategy, sustainability is a change in how we approach and value our resources.

The future of sustainable organizations is guided by relentless innovation, proactive leadership, and empowered employees who, while achieving organizational goals, also contribute to a grander vision of sustainable development.

As companies seek to position themselves as thought leaders and industry front-runners, more businesses will embrace the Sustainable Organization business model, and the journey towards a global sustainable future will keep getting stronger and brighter. True sustainability lies on the horizon, but every step we take today leads to a better tomorrow.

This chapter laid the foundation for understanding Sustainable

Organizations. The following chapters will delve deeper into how businesses can adopt and execute sustainable practices effectively to bring rewarding changes. We will explore the tools, techniques, and best practices championed by inspirational enterprises that have balanced growth with sustainability. The goal is to empower you with the knowledge and tools to create or transform an organization that operates sustainably.

Chapter 3. Eco-Enlightened Workforce: The Role of Employees in Sustainable Organizations

Across the corporate cosmos, an awakening is occurring. At the crossroads of business strategies and environmental consciousness, the workforce is emerging as a potent force, serving as a catalyst in the quest for sustainability. Amidst this rapidly shifting business matrix, the personnel arena has turned into a laboratory, constantly experimenting, adapting, and delivering innovative solutions to tackle mounting environmental challenges, simultaneously weaving sustainability into the very fabric of organizations.

3.1. The Core Constituents: Employees

In considering the transformative potential of a sustainable organization, it's incumbent on us to first appreciate its core elements, its employees. They are the gears that keep the machine of progress moving forward, the human component that actualizes vision into impact. Realizing the green revolution at workplace is something that goes beyond directives, it resides in the hearts and minds of these individuals.

Increasingly, company leaders recognize the imperative to engage employees, not just as functionaries, but as active partners, contributing their insights, ideas, and initiatives to progressively reimagine the corporate environment. To engender this wave of empowering eco-consciousness, organizations need to fuel a culture where employees are inspired, trained, encouraged, and rewarded for their eco-initiatives, transforming them into sustainability champions.

3.2. Toward a Greener Mindset: Education and Training

Knowledge is power, and this rings particularly true when it comes to promoting sustainability. Corporations that prioritize the education of their workforce on matters of environmental impact reassure employees about the sincerity of the organization's sustainability goals. Upskilling and reskilling activities could include workshops, seminars, webinars, interactive sessions, and more, ensuring a robust grasp of green strategies among the workforce.

Such training should cover an array of topics, breaking down corporate sustainability goals into quantifiable actions, explaining the environmental implications of their everyday work, emphasizing energy efficiency, resource management, and waste segregation. It's essential to shine a light on the direct link between their day-to-day roles and the potential for positive environmental impact.

3.3. Green Advocacy: Policies and Performance Metrics

Creating an eco-friendly business culture isn't limited to imparting knowledge. It also requires incorporating environmentally-focused performance metrics into employee evaluation systems. By recognizing and rewarding eco-conscious conduct, organizations can motivate employees towards active participation.

Inclusion of green metrics in appraisal systems could encompass various parameters: Contribution to energy-saving initiatives, sustainable project management, reductions in waste generation, frequency of 'green' suggestions made, and innovative ideas proposed for boosting sustainability. Building these matrices into the reward system forms an integral part of the culturally transformative framework of the organization.

3.4. The Power of Participation

One of the crucial ingredients for breathing life into this eco-enlightened paradigm is fostering a sense of collective ownership and emotional investment among employees. "Inclusive decision-making" isn't just a buzzword; it's a reality that constantly shapes the corporate sustainability landscape. When employees contribute to shaping the organization's sustainability strategy, it becomes not just a company venture, but "our venture."

To capitalize on this force, companies can establish platforms like sustainability suggestion boxes, feedback sessions, and 'green committees.' These platforms provide avenues for employees to voice their views, provide suggestions, debate possible solutions, and influence the organization's operating path towards sustainability.

3.5. Stories of Success: Case Studies

To further boost employee morale and offer a tangible portrayal of what they can achieve, shining a spotlight on successful case studies within the organization is invaluable. These real-life examples of green initiatives and their results serve as compelling evidence of the difference each individual can make when they step up to the sustainability challenge. They inspire action, showcasing the power of collective environmental consciousness.

3.6. Conclusion: A Symbiotic Symphony

The creation of a sustainable organization isn't an act of solitary significance but a harmonic concert composed of countless micro-actions resonating together. It's an orchestra in which every employee is an indispensable instrument, playing its part in this grand symphony of sustainability.

In this transforming environment, the emerging role of the 'eco-enlightened' workforce is pivotal. It represents a fundamental shift from a traditional top-down model to an empowering ecosphere, where decisions and actions prosper in a fertile ground of innovation, green cultural norms, and shared goals. Employees are indeed becoming the backbone of this transformative pathway towards a greener future, proving that the journey towards sustainability is collective, shared, and driven by unified resolve.

In the spirit of inexorable progress, let this be an invitation, a call-to-arms for businesses across the globe to empower their workforce in becoming architects of a sustainable tomorrow. By harnessing the power of the enlightened eco-workforce, we are not just reaffirming our commitment to a sustainable future but actively shaping it, one green decision at a time.

Indeed, the "green revolution" in the workplace has begun, and it's the employees leading the way, proving that it truly pays to play green.

Chapter 4. Unveiling the Green Giants: Case Studies of Sustainable Organizations

The Industrial Revolution marked the beginning of a new era, offering immense gains at the cost of widespread environmental devastation. Today, as we grapple with the consequences, it is clear that profitable enterprises can no longer wreak havoc on our planet. Progressive organizations are acknowledging the existential crisis of climate change and transitioning into sustainable entities. Moving beyond a singular profit-driven focus, these pioneers are embedding sustainability into their core functioning. Let's initiate our discourse with a focus on some of these green giants.

4.1. Starbucks: Pioneering Sustainable Coffee Practices

Starbucks as a corporate entity has been driving sustainability for over two decades now. Being a coffee-retail giant, the company acknowledged the metamorphic potential of implementing sustainable practices in its global operations.

The commitment to sustainability goes beyond the stores and touches upon every aspect of the supply chain. Starbucks ensures the coffee they sell is ethically sourced and accredited by external bodies like Conservation International. The company's strategy called 'Coffee and Farmer Equity (C.A.F.E.) Practices' sets ethical and sustainable standards for sourcing, supporting farmers in over 30 countries.

Another significant step has been towards reducing the environmental impact through redesigning and innovating on product packaging. Starbucks made a pledge to phase out plastic straws by 2020 and transition to strawless lids, thereby mitigating a significant source of non-recyclable waste.

4.2. Google: Powering Tech with Green Energy

In the digital world, Google stands out as a beacon of sustainability. It has continually adopted practices that achieve business growth while reducing carbon footprint, symbolizing the symbiotic relationship between profit and sustainability.

Google achieved 100% renewable energy for its global operations in 2017. It has taken up the ambition to operate carbon-free entirely by 2020 and is making significant investments in wind and solar farms across the world. Google is also on track to neutralize carbon emissions entirely for all its past operations by purchasing high-quality carbon offsets.

Apart from that, Google uses advanced AI to improve the efficiency of its data centers, with a focus on reducing its energy use. Nest, Google's smart thermostat, also enables users to reduce their carbon footprint, showcasing how technology can be a catalyst for sustainability.

4.3. Patagonia: Embedding Sustainability in Business Model

An outdoor clothing retailer, Patagonia, has turned the retail industry's typical business model on its head by reinventing itself as a purpose-driven brand focused on sustainability.

Firstly, Patagonia uses recycled materials in two-thirds of its product line. They initiated the 'Worn Wear' program, which encourages customers to repair their Patagonia gear rather than replace it. They also introduce the responsible economy concept, urging consumers to buy only what they need and reduce wastage.

Moreover, Patagonia is part of the 1% for the Planet alliance, pledging to donate 1% of its sales to the preservation and restoration of the natural environment.

4.4. Interface: Revolutionizing Carpet Industry

Interface, a global commercial flooring company, has achieved its 'Mission Zero' goal by 2020, creating a carbon-neutral product portfolio.

Since 1994, the company has been driven by a mission to eliminate any negative impact by the firm on the environment through aggressive and visionary targets. They have achieved a 96% reduction in greenhouse gas emissions, 89% reduction in waste to landfill and 88% water use reduction since 1996.

They have also implemented a 'ReEntry' program, where existing products are repurposed to create new ones, hence embodying the circular economy concept.

4.5. IKEA: Designing Sustainable Solutions

IKEA has set ambitious aims to become fully circular and climate positive by 2030. Sustainability is entrenched into the designs of IKEA, with a majority of products now being made of renewable, recyclable or recycled materials.

It has committed to making all its products comply with circular design principles by 2030 - which means they should be designed from the start for reuse, repair, repurposing or recycling.

IKEA has also established itself as a renewable energy enterprise having invested in wind farms and solar power in a bid to reduce its carbon footprint. As of 2020, IKEA produced more renewable energy than it consumes in its operations.

These organizations are proof that it's possible to blend profit with eco-affability. The transformative, self-enforced changes these corporations have made to their business models and operations have set robust precedents, raising the sustainability bar for their industries. These 'Green Giants' underscore the reality that initiative, commitment, and innovation can indeed help in striking a balance between commercial success and environmental responsibility.

As we tread ahead in our exploration of sustainable organizations, these insightful real-life narratives provide a strong groundwork upon which to construct the future chapters. The road towards a sustainable future involves comprehensive change - a revamping of traditional business models, practices, and mindsets; these inspiring stories reflect the changing corporate landscape, signaling towards a greener horizon.

Chapter 5. Grassroots to the C-Suite: Empowering Green Decision Making at All Levels

The story of sustainability in contemporary organizations is far from crystallized at the top echelons of management. A sustainable future necessitates democratizing the green decision-making process, ensuring that it percolates down from the C-Suite to the grassroots. This chapter delves into this journey, exploring the nuances of systemic shifts and individualistic stewardship in making the eco-friendly leap.

5.1. Understanding Empowerment in Eco-decisions

Empowerment in corporate vernacular is not merely assigning tasks, but rather ensuring that employees at all levels are sufficiently provided with the knowledge, skill set, and agency to make effective decisions. When it comes to environmental sustainability, this means fostering a culture that encourages awareness about eco-friendly practices, sparks creative problem-solving regarding environmental concerns, and instills a sense of responsibility towards being stewards of the environment.

Empowerment manifests itself at two intersections - the systemic and individualistic. The former revolves around formal strategies and practices designed by the organization to foster eco-friendly decisions. Simultaneously, individualistic empowerment emphasizes the role of employees in driving these initiatives, allowing them to take localized decisions aligned with the larger sustainable strategy.

5.2. Systemic Empowerment

Organizations worldwide are now constructing an eco-system that encourages and supports green decision-making. They are embedding sustainability into their strategic planning, operational processes, and performance evaluation metrics. This involves incorporating environmental considerations in product designing, sourcing, manufacturing, packaging, and distribution.

Companies are also fostering eco-friendly behavior among employees through clear and consistent communication about their environmental mission. In-house workshops, webinars, knowledge-sharing platforms, and e-learning modules are frequently utilized to promote such awareness. Furthermore, many organizations have started including sustainability-related targets in their performance appraisals, thereby aligning employee goals with the firm's green ambitions.

5.3. Individualistic Empowerment

Individualistic empowerment often operates on a grassroot level, prioritizing the sense of ownership and responsibility among employees towards their firm's environmental mission. Encouraging creative problem-solving, recognizing and rewarding green initiatives, and promoting peer-to-peer teaching are some ways through which these organizations aim to build eco-leaders across verticals.

The advantages of bottom-up empowerment are twofold. Firstly, employees from different roles and functions, fueled by their unique perspectives and experiences, can suggest creative and functional solutions for environmental challenges. Secondly, by taking part in these green initiatives, they develop a sense of ownership and are more likely to adopt eco-consciousness in their professional and personal lives.

5.4. Case Studies

To illustrate empowerment in eco-decision making, let's recount two successful stories. The first is from Xanterra Travel Collection, an American company specializing in environmentally responsible travel experiences. Xanterra adopted an employee-centric approach, leveraging its workforce's creativity to lead environmental problem-solving. Through digital platforms, workshops, and forums, it encouraged employees to propose innovative solutions to reduce their environmental footprint. As a result, numerous small but significant changes were introduced in their operations leading to enormous cumulative impact.

Meanwhile, Patagonia, the outdoor clothing brand, instills responsible consumption ethos in employees through policies and practices. It has adopted measures, such as offering repair services to increase product longevity, launching a resale platform for used Patagonia products, and incorporating recycled materials in its product design. By enabling their employees to be part of the solution, they transformed into ambassadors of environmental sustainability.

5.5. From Grassroots to the C-Suite: Key Takeaways

Empowering green decision-making at all levels necessitates that organizations adopt both top-down and bottom-up approach. They need to fold sustainability into their DNA through an ecosystem that supports such values and inspire their employees to be a proactive part of this journey. Empowerment requires education, encouragement, and enabling employees to ideate, innovate, and implement green practices. The resultant eco-consciousness not only aids the environment but also contributes significantly to the organization's growth and reputation.

As actors in success stories have shown, when powered appropriately, every employee right from the grassroots becomes instrumental to the green symphony that the most advanced C-Suites are trying to orchestrate. This ecosystem of empowerment fosters a sustainable corporate culture, where every small step towards environmental stewardship paves the way for a robust policy framework and ignites transformative green initiatives.

In conclusion, the journey from grassroots to the C-Suite is interconnected, iterative, and must be inclusive. For only when every cog in the corporate wheel thinks, acts, and operates sustainably can we envision a brighter, greener future. Hence, consider this a clarion call for organizations to democratize sustainability, ensure that every employee is armed, equipped, and inspired to make green decisions, so that together we can rewrite the future of our planet.

Chapter 6. The Power of Policy: Nurturing a Culture of Sustainability

Policies are the steering wheel that drive the course of an organization, marking the path for its growth and development. In the context of sustainability, they become even more pivotal, as they frame the environment in which sustainable behaviors flourish.

6.1. At The Helm: Leadership and Sustainable Policies

Leadership plays a critical role in shaping the course of sustainability policies. The roots of sustainable practices extend from the top-floor offices to the shop-floor employees; they are embedded in an organization's DNA by its leaders. Leaders should strive to live by the principles of sustainability and set an example for their teams. Their commitment to sustainable practices induces a trickle-down effect, nurturing a pro-environment ethos throughout the organization.

Leading through sustainable policies involves the broad vision of integrating sustainability objectives into the core of an organization's strategies. These policies can include energy-efficient operational methods, reduced usage of natural resources, waste minimization, and fostering an environmentally conscious culture.

6.2. The Cornerstones: Designing Effective Sustainability Policies

For a sustainability policy to work, it must be practical, feasible, and rewarding. The policy provides the structural outline within which the organization operates, highlighting the behaviors that are deemed appropriate and important by the organization.

Clarity: Effective sustainability policies should be clear and straightforward. Ambiguity could lead to misinterpretation, thereby diluting the impact of the policy. Policies should be accurately communicated to all involved, ensuring everyone understands the expectations and objectives of the initiatives.

Inclusivity: A good policy involves employees at each level of the organization, ensuring that everyone's voice is heard. This promotes buy-in and ownership, key elements to the success of sustainability initiatives.

Scalability: Policies must be scalable. As the organization expands, the policies should adapt and evolve, fostering a sustainable foundation that can accommodate growth while preserving its core values.

Accountability: Any effective policy includes mechanisms for monitoring and enforcing the policy. This may involve regular audits, feedback loops, ongoing monitoring and measurement systems, and recognizing or rewarding compliance.

6.3. The Framework: Laws and Regulations

The environmental awakening on a global scale has led to the establishment of numerous environmental laws and regulations. These provide the legislative framework within which companies must operate. To foster a culture of sustainability, there is a pressing need for familiarization and adherence to these laws and regulations.

These legislative tools act as external enforcers of sustainability policies. They ensure that organizations are accountable for their actions by imposing penalties for non-compliance, providing an additional motivational layer for organizations to adopt sustainable practices.

Understanding, interpreting, and complying with these laws can be daunting. Organizations can consider leveraging the expertise of environmental legal advisors to guide them through this process, ensuring that they remain compliant and updated about the latest changes in environmental law.

6.4. The Execution: Implementing Sustainable Policies

Crafting a sustainable policy is just one half of the equation - it's the implementation that brings the policy to life. Successful implementation can be facilitated by weaving sustainability into the very essence of the company's culture and encouraging "green" behavior at each organizational level.

The first step toward implementing a policy is to communicate it effectively to all employees, making sure everyone is aware of the policy and understands its importance, implications, and their role within it.

Next, there is a dire need for training and development programs targeted at teaching employees the necessary skills to adhere to sustainability policies. This involves practical sessions wherein employees can understand the environmental consequences of their routine activities, spurring them to instill a green approach in their work.

Finally, regularly revisiting and revising the sustainability policies is crucial. The dynamics of the world are changing constantly, and what was viable yesterday might not be the same today. Hence, a continuous reassessment of the policies helps mold them according to the ever-evolving environmental panorama, keeping the sustainability efforts relevant and effective.

6.5. The Impact: A Tangible Shift in Culture

Over time, with the correct design, implementation and reinforcement, these sustainable policies become ingrained into the organizational culture. They shape employees' behaviors, decisions, and attitudes, creating an environment supportive of sustainability.

When employees witness concrete results derived from their efforts, it boosts their morale and fuels their drive to perform better. An effective reward and recognition system also goes a long way in reinforcing the values of sustainability and creating a culture of reverence towards nature.

By nurturing a culture of sustainability, companies not only contribute positively to the environment, but they also contribute to an improved brand image and reputation, enhanced employee satisfaction, and overall increased stakeholder value.

To conclude, policies play a monumental role in ushering in a sustainable existence within an organization. The importance of leadership commitment, policy design, adherence to regulations, effective execution, and continual reassessment cannot be stressed enough. These are, after all, the pillars that bring the purpose of sustainability to life within an organization, manifesting as a tangible shift in culture that permeates every layer of the business. Thus, the power of policy in nurturing a culture of sustainability is undeniable, immeasurable, and absolutely critical.

Chapter 7. Toolkits for Transformation: Resources to Empower Eco-Conscious Choices

Stepping into the realm of environmental sustainability within organizations beckons a shift in dynamics - a shift wherein each individual, from entry-level employees to the C-suite, becomes an active and empowered participant in the company's eco-sustainable journey. To facilitate this transformation and foster the successful implementation of green strategies, we need to arm our employees with the right tools, knowledge, and motivation. These toolkits are crucial in creating a culture of informed, eco-conscious choices in organizations.

7.1. A Green Education:

Empowering green choices begins with an understanding of the environment and our impact on it. Thankfully, much research has been done, published, and compiled, rendering accessible learning materials for companies to leverage.

Companies can introduce comprehensive training programs that not only relate to the employees' immediate job role but also extend to wider environmental implications. Online courses are abundant on platforms such as Coursera, Udemy, and Google's Your Plan, Your Planet, amongst others. Webinars, workshops, seminars - be they physically on location or digitally - also offer expertise on different aspects of environmental awareness, carbon footprint, renewable energy sources, and much more.

7.2. Fostering a Culture of Eco-Consciousness:

Creating a culture of environmental concern isn't just about disseminating information but ensuring it sinks into the organizational fabric and impacts decision-making processes.

In this endeavor, companies could benefit greatly from Employee Volunteer Programs (EVPs). These promote an empathetic understanding of the environment by offering firsthand experiences of contributing to sustainability projects, fostering a sense of 'eco-pride' amongst employees.

Case sharing also proves fruitful, where employees are invited to brainstorm and implement green-ideas within the organizational operational scope. They can, then, take stock of the practical implications of their choices, fostering real, palpable environmental awareness.

7.3. Tracking Environmental Footprint:

Remember, 'What gets measured, gets managed.'

Tools such as carbon calculators, water footprint tools, and waste tracking systems can be instrumental in not only monitoring the environmental footprint but also evaluating the organization's progress and identifying areas of improvement.

For example, platforms like Metrio and Greenstone offer accurate tracking of companies' environmental footprints and offer actionable insights based on the data. These analytics can be cascaded down to individual employees for their understanding and contribution to reducing the footprint.

7.4. Frameworks and Certifications:

Various internationally recognized environmental management frameworks, such as ISO 14001, are ready blueprints that companies can follow to navigate their sustainable journey.

Companies can take it a step further by forging alliances with ethical and sustainable certification bodies for product-making processes. Fairtrade, Rainforest Alliance, Organic - these labels not only magnify the company's dedication to green values but serve as visual reminders for employees to align with these values.

7.5. Technology and Digital Tools:

Technological advancements have paved the way for numerous digital tools that facilitate the integration of sustainable practices into daily workflows.

Software like EnergyCAP, for energy management, My Waste App, for waste management, Dynamizer, to manage and visualize sustainability data - provide not only company-wide solutions but, in some instances, can also be personalized to individual roles and responsibilities.

7.6. Friendly Competition:

Never underestimate the power of friendly competition to encourage participation and enthusiasm.

Incentivizing greener choices by introducing eco-ratings, leaderboards, and competitions can prove effective. You could identify unique awards or recognitions like "Green Innovator of the Month" or "Eco-Friendly Department" which are fun and motivational. Such initiatives foster a sense of camaraderie while instilling a deep passion for sustainable practices.

In sum, the marriage of information with involvement creates transformative change. With strategic know-how, effective tools, and a genuine passion for sustainability, organizations can confidently stride on the path of environmental sustainability. Embrace these toolkits for transformation and ensure every choice made within the organization is made in the best interest of our environment.

Chapter 8. Education to Empower: Training Programs for Sustainable Action

Knowledge is the necessary scaffold upon which we build impactful changes. And nowhere is the need for rigorous and comprehensive education more apparent than in the realms of environmental sustainability and corporate social responsibility. Adoption of sustainable practices holds wonderful promise; yet, it demands a shift not just for organizations but also for the employees who create the rhythmic hum of daily operations.

8.1. A New Learning Paradigm

The education process begins with a thoughtful challenge and redefinition of the existing norms. More than just addition of new knowledge, it entails reinterpretation and reframing of the existing one. Here, individuals must understand why they need to abandon old, unsustainable techniques in favour of more eco-responsive alternatives. By forging a direct connection between the employees' actions and their environmental impacts, organizations can create compelling reasons for behavioural change.

Consider the simple act of reducing paper waste in the office. Instead of mandating a paperless environment or just hinting at the desired behaviour, education must anchor itself in clear context. Employees could learn about the entire lifecycle of the paper - ranging from the deforestation involved to the pollutants released during the recycling process. With this, the act of saving paper morphs from a vague edict into a conscious action, capable of making a tangible difference.

In this regard, the educational initiatives must be a continuous journey rather than a one-time event. Persistent reinforcement can come in various forms - whether it is reminder posters on office walls, setting monthly 'Green' KPIs or incorporating sustainability missions in the performance review.

8.2. Training in Action

Implementing a training program whilst building an environment that fosters sustainable thinking are no trifling ordeals. Nevertheless, firms that have ventured into this profoundly impactful journey showcase the rewards are worth the labour.

A major global clothing retailer, for example, introduced "Green Warriors", a program consisting of seminars, workshops, and group exercises intended to expedite the shift towards sustainability. The training events had participation across all levels - from warehouse workers to top management. Within two years of launching the initiative, the company reported a significant decrease in material waste, water usage, and carbon emissions.

Likewise, an energy giant took a multi-faceted approach in training its staff. It began with a remarkable feat of introducing Augmented Reality (AR) in training sessions, where participants visualized the carbon emission statistics attributed to the firm. This was complemented by regular workshops and online webinars on alternative energy sources, carbon capture, and fuel efficiency. Two years and over 45 thousand trained employees later, the company publicly announced a 20% reduction in carbon emissions.

Examples like these bring home the immense transformative power of thorough training programs.

8.3. Creating Measurable Learning Outcomes

In ensuring the effectiveness of the training program, objective measures of the learning outcomes are by no means less important than the content itself. They not only unmask the gray area between theoretical knowledge and practical application, but also serve as a feedback loop into refining the training itself.

Appropriate measures could be a combination of qualitative and quantitative parameters. These may range from 'before and after surveys' to capture change in awareness & attitude, usage data of resources (like paper, water, energy) at department-level to track behaviour changes. Moreover, encouraging employees to set personal sustainability goals and documenting their progress could be a very potent way to foster intrinsic motivation.

8.4. Conclusion

Education and empowerment are the lighthouses illuminating the path towards corporate sustainability. They enhance the canvas of possibilities, assisting employees to conceive and execute impactful green decisions.

As we delve deeper into recognizing the short-term and long-term effects of our every decision, we inculcate a thought-provoking dialogue within our workspaces. Employees, when driven by purpose and equipped with the right skills, can become the potent change agents for environmental sustainability. Consequently, educating and empowering teams is not just an investment in corporate vision but indeed, an investment to secure the future of our planet.

Chapter 9. Measuring Green Success: The Metrics of Sustainability

Green metrics or sustainability metrics stand as the cornerstone in gaiving real-time insights and enabling organizations to refine their eco techniques. These metrics not only indicate performance against sustainability goals but also place organizations in a superior position to disclose their environmental footprints and foster longevity.

9.1. Understanding Sustainability Metrics

Sustainability metrics provide the concrete measurements necessary to gauge the eco-impact of a business. They are quantities derived from data that represents a particular aspect of sustainability, providing an organization a means of self-assessment. Sustainability metrics are designed to be direct, easy-to-understand indicators that can be universally applied to any aspect of business operation.

Organizations may encounter a wide array of sustainability metrics, each applicable to different areas. Environmental metrics, for instance, measure impact such as greenhouse gas emissions, water usage, and waste production. Economic metrics focus more on business sustainability, measuring factors such as profitability and revenue growth. Social metrics touch on the quality of workforce experience, like employee health and safety, equality, and diversity. Each metric is underpinned by a set of norms and standardization measures that help organizations to monitor their progress and chart their journey toward sustainability.

9.2. The Role of Sustainability Metrics in Business Decision-Making

Sustainability metrics can function as a critical compass on an organization's eco journey, informing strategic decision-making and operational planning. Through sustainability metrics, businesses have a tangible means of monitoring their performance against set targets, revealing where their strategies may be failing and suggesting areas of improvement.

Indeed, sustainability metrics can stimulate reevaluation and catalyze innovation, pushing companies to venture beyond traditional methods and forge ahead towards novel, eco-conscious solutions. Crucially, these metrics also foster transparency, allowing businesses to communicate their sustainability progress with their stakeholders — an increasingly important factor in today's climate-conscious world.

9.3. Key Sustainability Metrics to Measure

While innumerable sustainability metrics are available, a select few tend to stand out in their relevance and utility. We must emphasize, however, the importance of customizing these metrics to individual organizational needs — a one-size-fits-all approach is inadequate, given the diverse nature of businesses and their varying impacts on the environment.

1. **Carbon Footprint**: This is the total greenhouse gas emissions caused directly or indirectly by an organization, measured in units of carbon dioxide. It is regarded as one of the essential indicators of environmental impact.

2. **Water Footprint**: The total volume of freshwater consumed, polluted, or wasted is known as the water footprint. It provides a comprehensive overview of an organization's water usage, including its supply-chain.

3. **Energy Consumption**: Amount and type of energy used in an organization's operations is a vital metric, often divided into non-renewable and renewable energy usage.

4. **Waste Generation**: This accounts for the total waste generated, including solid, liquid, gaseous, hazardous, and non-hazardous waste.

5. **Supply-chain Sustainability**: Measures the extent to which sustainability principles are considered and implemented in an organization's supply chain.

9.4. Quantifying and Maturing your Green Success

However, merely identifying and measuring these metrics isn't enough. There needs to be a concerted effort to improve these metrics over time iteratively. Consistent monitoring, reporting, and progression underpin the realization of genuine sustainability.

Moreover, establishing effective communication channels to relay these improvements to a broader audience — stakeholders, customers, and employees — can not only bolster an organization's brand image but also stimulate a ripple effect that propels others in its sphere towards sustainable action.

9.5. Benchmarking Success with the Global Reporting Initiative

To ensure uniformity in sustainability metrics, organizations can use frameworks such as the Global Reporting Initiative (GRI). The GRI Standards create a common language for organizations to report sustainability issues, thus enabling concrete comparisons and benchmarking.

Today, GRI is widely regarded as a global best practice for reporting on a range of economic, environmental, and social impacts. Alignment with GRI ensures a business's sustainability efforts are both globally recognized and effectively comparable against industry peers, further fostering sustainable growth.

9.6. Closure

Clearly, sustainability metrics serve more than a quantitive purpose. They drive businesses towards continuous eco-improvement, shaping systemic changes within the organization. By mastering the art of measuring green success, organizations can ensure their part in paving the path to a sustainable future is significant, and hard to ignore. For it is only through measurement, we can manage our ecological impact and strive for finer sustainability frontiers.

Chapter 10. Challenges and Solutions: Navigating the Path Towards Sustainability

Every journey begins with the first step, and the trek towards sustainability is no exception. Employees are being tasked with a significant role in initiating and maintaining green practices in their respective workplaces. This initially presents both unique challenges and viable solutions, setting a momentum that can make or break the course to a sustainable future.

10.1. Understanding the Challenges

Before plunging into the solutions, it's essential to grasp the breadth and depth of the challenges that organizations face when moving towards sustainability. A clear understanding of these obstacles serves as the starting point to map out tailor-fit solutions.

1. Lack of Awareness and Education

The foremost hurdle is the dearth of understanding and awareness about sustainability. Many employees are oblivious to the pressing need for sustainable practices and the role they could play. Instead, they primarily concentrate on their job-specific tasks, leaving environmental problems at large for others to tackle.

1. Resource Allocation

Dedicating investments and resources towards sustainability initiatives poses a significant challenge for many organizations. Businesses often view these investments as additional expenses, not considering the long-term paybacks they could reap from adopting sustainable practices.

1. Change Resistance

It's human nature to resist change, primarily when it disrupts established routines. As a consequence, adapting to eco-friendly practices often meets resistance from employees who struggle to break free from old habits and work patterns.

1. Inadequate Technology and Infrastructure

For successful execution of green practices, adequate technology and infrastructure are vital. Many organizations lack the advanced tools and infrastructure necessary for handling complex aspects of sustainability, be it waste management, energy efficiency, or emissions reduction.

1. Unclear Regulations

Fluctuating and often conflicting regulations also pose a challenge. Clear, cohesive, and stable policies regarding sustainability can help companies plan and execute their initiatives efficiently.

10.2. Ingraining Sustainability: Potential Solutions

With the challenges identified, the next step is to devise potential solutions. Fostering sustainability is not a one-off task, but a journey that requires culture change, practical policies, and innovative strategies.

1. Awareness and Education Programs

Companies must initiate regular training sessions and workshops to educate employees about the role and importance of sustainable practices. Explaining how their individual actions can have a significant impact on the environment helps engender a sense of responsibility.

1. Strategic Investment and Budget Allocation

An effective way to overcome resource challenges is to allocate a reserved budget for sustainability endeavors. This can include investment in greener technology, infrastructure for waste management, and funding for training programs.

1. Incentives and Reward Systems

To alleviate resistance to change, companies could introduce incentives and reward systems that encourage sustainable behavior. Be it small rewards for reducing waste or recognition for championing a sustainability project— these gestures can motivate employees.

1. Adapting Technological Innovations

Organizations should consider investing in innovative technologies to manage their carbon footprint, improve waste disposal, and enhance energy use. This could involve upgrading machinery and office appliances to greener alternatives or leveraging digital platforms for remote collaboration to minimize travel and emissions.

1. Lobbying for Clearer Policies

Organizations can join hands with industry peers and lobby for the development of clear and stable sustainability regulations. Uniform guidelines will provide a level playing field where companies can innovate without regulatory risks.

10.3. Reaping the Benefits of Sustainability

A focus on sustainability drives not only environmental benefits but also significant advantages for the organizations themselves. Improved reputation, customer loyalty, cost savings, and enhanced employee satisfaction are just a few paybacks from embracing sustainability. As more and more businesses step into the world of sustainable practices, it's not just about the singular act of adopting green measures; it's about redefining growth and business success in an era of environmental consciousness.

Heading towards a sustainable future invites both challenges and rewards. However, with the right strategies in place, the journey can be less daunting and more rewarding. At the heart of it lies the core principle: empowering employees to be the torchbearers of change, leading their organizations towards a sustainable future.

Chapter 11. Looking Ahead: The Future of Work in Sustainable Organizations

The fascinating journey of sustainable organizations does not culminate at the mere adoption of eco-friendly practices, but continues as a constant evolution with the changing fabric of our socio-economic environment. As we delve into this evolving landscape, we must elucidate the future of work in these organizations as it is intrinsically woven into the very premise of sustainability.

11.1. A Brighter, Greener Outlook

The future of work in sustainable organizations presents a brighter, greener outlook - one that focuses on the integration of environmental, social, and governance (ESG) considerations into business strategies. While this vision has been gaining momentum over the years, it is likely to command mainstream focus in the coming years. Businesses are experiencing a paradigm shift, and economic viability is seen through the lens of sustainability now, more than ever.

To put this into perspective, Deloitte's Global Human Capital Trends survey, 2020, illustrates that nearly 80% of the 9,000 surveyed executives believe that corporate sustainability initiatives will result in substantial changes to their business operations. This heralds the advent of a new age that attempts to harmonize environmental and business sustainability, propelling us towards a future where 'profit with a purpose' becomes the mainstay of corporate ethos.

11.2. Harnessing Talent With Torches of Sustainability

A component integral to the future of work in sustainable organizations is the evolution of talent management strategies. Organizations are casting their nets wider, looking beyond skill-based competencies when hiring employees. The aspiration to attract sustainability-conscious workforce arises from a cognizance that such individuals are likely to be innovative problem solvers and intrinsically motivated.

This reflects the changing dynamic of what employees and job seekers value - companies with a clear response to climate change, water scarcity, and other environmental threats are found to be more appealing. They stimulate the workforce's potential, stirring a sense of purpose, motivation and engagement that inevitably leads to noteworthy entrepreneurial outcomes.

11.3. Technology: The Enabler and Catalyzer

Emphasizing the role of technology in the future of work in sustainable organizations, it is the driving force behind the ability to expand operations without expanding environmental footprints. Balancing growth and sustainability becomes possible through embracing digital transformation, harnessing AI, advanced analytics, IoT, and blockchain.

For instance, many global brands are extensively utilizing AI and machine learning to predict and minimize their energy consumption patterns, thereby reducing their carbon footprints. In manufacturing settings, IoT enabled devices are contributing to the objective of reducing waste and enhancing resource efficiency. This technology-enabled vision converges on 'doing well by doing good', proving both economic and environmental gains.

11.4. Educating for Sustainability

Institutions, whether educational or corporate, have a critical role to play in nurturing a generation geared towards problem-solving concerns around sustainability. Curriculum development that intertwines economic feasibility, environmental stewardship and social responsibility can unravel the nuances of sustainability and the future of work.

This conscious shift towards sustainability literacy is reflected in an increasing number of MBA programs offering dedicated sustainability modules. The adoption of these modules is indicative of the burgeoning demand for sustainability-oriented skills and business acumen among future corporate leaders.

11.5. Diverse Yet Inclusive: The Sustainable Corporate Environment

Workplace diversity and inclusivity are potent signals demonstrating an organization's commitment to sustainability. Companies maintaining a diverse workforce of varying genders, races, ages, and backgrounds are likely to represent a wider array of perspectives. This diversity could catalyze innovative approaches to environmental and social challenges.

Moreover, inclusivity traditionally fosters a sense of belonging and empowers employees on an individual level. When the focus of that empowerment shifts towards sustainability efforts, the collective force can charge the durability of a company's eco-conscious strategies.

In conclusion, examining the projected landscape of these workplaces, it is clear that the future of work in sustainable organizations is dynamic, inclusive, technologically advanced and educationally empowering. These traits present an optimistic narrative that sustainable actions are no longer relegated to the fringes of corporate policy, but are becoming an essential part of the main discourse. The focus is shifting from 'could we?' to 'how can we?', driving sustainable organizations towards a transformative path where growth and responsibility coexist.

www.ingramcontent.com/pod-product-compliance
Lightning Source LLC
Chambersburg PA
CBHW062310290526
45794CB00006B/2743